Ripley's Believe It or Not!

OUT OF THIS WORLD EDITION 2018

Scholastic Inc.

101

Contents

19

48

99

Who Is Robert Ripley?

Robert Ripley shared the unbelievable with scores of adoring fans, but he started with just pen and paper. He began working as a cartoonist at the *New York Globe* newspaper in 1913, quickly turning his sports cartoon *Champs and Chumps* into the world-famous *Believe It or Not!*

Ripley visited more than 200 countries in his lifetime, covering 464,000 miles!

Ripley received more than a million letters a year—more mail than Santa Claus and U.S. presidents!

Cartoons

The Ripley cartoons are still drawn every day, making *Ripley's Believe It or Not!* the longest running syndicated cartoon in the world! These cartoons were drawn by Ripley's current cartoonist, John Graziano, who sent his drawings to Ripley's as a teenager before getting the job years later.

The Ripley's Believe It or Not!
Odditorium in Niagara Falls,
Canada, after its recent
external renovation.

Today the Ripley's team carries on his
legacy, hunting for the best "believe it or
nots!" from around the world. We gather
facts from many different sources—but some
of the most incredible stories are still sent
to us personally from our Ripley fans.

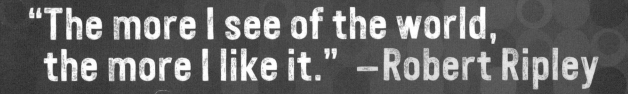

"The more I see of the world,
the more I like it." –Robert Ripley

Straight from the Ripley Warehouse...

Ripley's archivist Edward Meyer, based in our head office in Orlando, Florida, spends most of his year looking for new and unique exhibits for all our Ripley's Believe It or Not! Odditoriums. Here are just a few of the amazing pieces he has bought this year, straight from the Ripley warehouse . . .

Created by Doug Powell, this computer keyboard portrait of Princess Leia includes hidden names like CHEWBACCA, REY, and BB-8.

This figure of Darth Vader by Gabriel Dishaw of Fishers, Indiana, is made from computer parts, adding machines, and typewriters.

Built by a Justin La Doux of Alma, Michigan, this tiger is made of recycled metal.

Check out some of these amazing stories inside your book...

Incredible!

Keep on an eye out for more Ripley stories and fascinating facts!

PAGE 47

PAGE 84

Q+A

Watch out for interviews inside!

PAGE 104

If you have a story you think Ripley's would like, get in touch!

Write to **BION Research, Ripley Entertainment Inc.,** 7576 Kingspointe Parkway, Suite 188, Orlando, Florida, 32819, USA.

Include photos if you can!

CHAPTER 1

Peculiar Planet

Yoga Shutterbug

Elad Itzkin has two passions: photography and yoga. He combines them by practicing the art of yoga photography. From city streets to the Bahamas, Elad has photographed yoga models all over the world. He even snapped a yogi posing in the snowy caves of Iceland!

Charming Abodes

Shell House

A resident of Qingdao in China has decorated his house with over one million colored shells, completely covering the outside walls. It took two years and five hundred different types of shells, all of which he collected himself off the nearby beach.

Strange Brew

In 2006, Chinese artist Gu Yuezi moved to a jungle in southern China. No ordinary home would do for this unconventional thinker. Gu built a house shaped like a teapot—in a tree. The tea tree house features a dining hall, a bedroom, a bathroom, and a kitchen. His nearby art studio is shaped like a bird's nest.

Iraq's Tigris-Euphrates marshlands were once home to half a million Ma'dan tribespeople, or "Marsh Arabs," who lived in floating "basket" homes made entirely from reeds.

Architect David Hertz designed a luxury home called the "Wing House" in Malibu, California, using scrap material from an old Boeing 747 plane.

Amazing Athletics

Fire Football

As a reward for finishing their studies, students at a boarding school in Indonesia celebrate with a game of fire football. The game is played by soaking a coconut in kerosene and lighting it ablaze. Players don't even wear shoes!

→ Five **STRANGE SPORTS**

1 **HEAVY LIFTING** Participants in the Scottish Highland Games' iconic caber toss must pick up a log vertically and chuck it as far as they can.

2 **STIFF COMPETITION** Competitors at the shin kicking championships held at the Cotswold Olimpick Games in England grab onto their opponent's shoulders and kick each other's shins until one of them falls over.

3 **GOAT GRAB** Buzkashi is a centuries-old Central Asian sport during which players on horseback try to be the first to grab a headless goat carcass and carry it to the other end of the field.

4 **SWEET MOVES** Taking dog training to the next level is the rising sport of musical canine freestyle, where dog and owner join forces to perform and dance together.

5 **NO HANDS** Sepak takraw is a Southeast Asian game similar to volleyball, except the ball cannot be touched by hands or arms, resulting in spectacular kicks and flips.

Croc Cage

Adventurous visitors to Darwin, Australia, might try their hand at getting up close and personal with Australia's famous saltwater crocodiles. Crocosaurus Cove's Cage of Death is billed as "the only cage in the world that brings you face-to-face" with saltwater crocs in captivity. Just a clear, acrylic container is all that separates you from monster reptiles up to 16 feet long!

Colorful Surroundings

Psychedelic Salt Mines

The walls of these decommissioned salt mines in Yekaterinburg, Russia, are filled with multicolored hypnotic patterns. After years of digging into the mine, white, red, yellow, and blue layers of minerals now line miles of tunnel walls.

Balloon Rooms

More than one million balloons made up the 4-D Balloon Experience at Joy City in Tianjin, China. One room featured fluorescent inflatables glowing in the dark, while another was filled to the brim with white balloons resembling big, fluffy clouds. The exhibit also featured larger-than-life versions of cartoon characters and a long hallway decorated in arches that created a rainbow.

Head Work

Living Under a Rock

Nearly three thousand people live under the rocky overhangs of Setenil de las Bodegas in Spain. Though the cliff looks as if it could crush the town at any moment, people have been living under the stony cliffside for centuries.

Stilt Fishing

Fishermen in Galle, Sri Lanka, fish while balanced six feet above the water on stilts. The stilts are fixed to the seabed, and fishermen spend the hours of sunrise, noon, and sunset fishing from their elevated positions without even using bait.

Water Ways

Dinner on the Water

In a country with over one billion people, it can be hard to get away from it all and just have a romantic dinner. That's why a restaurant in Lin'an, China, serves guests on a floating platform that is only accessible by boat.

Floating Piers

For 16 days, a golden pier stretched out into Lake Iseo and framed the small island of Monte Isola in Italy. The project was conceived by artist Christo Vladimirov Yavachev and was made out of 220,000 foam cubes. The walkway allowed pedestrians to walk nearly 2 miles on top of the water.

Mario Kart

- Mario was named after Mario Segale, the Italian landlord of Nintendo of America's office, who bore a striking physical resemblance to the character.

- In 2013, a 10-year-old boy steered his great-grandmother's car to safety after she had a heart attack while driving. He credited his driving ability to playing Mario Kart Wii.

- Mario Kart 8 is the first game in the franchise to feature a fully animated mustache on Mario.

- Non-Nintendo characters Pac-Man, Ms. Pac-Man, and Blinky the Ghost were all playable characters in the oft-forgotten Mario Kart Arcade GP.

- You can actually buy a real-life Mario kart as seen in Mario Kart 7! Known as the Super Mario Kart Ride-On, the vehicle also features the full range of sound effects from the popular game.

- In the Japanese version of Mario Kart 64, the Moo Moo Farm course is called Moh Moh Farm, because in Japan, the "moo" sound cows make is more like "moh," with a long "o" sound.

- Thwomp's laughter in Mario Kart 64 is actually Wario's laugh slowed down.

- In Mario Kart 64, letting the music on the results screen loop 64 times (roughly 50 minutes) causes the music to change, playing an alternate hidden version of the "results" theme.

- In Mario Kart 7, the clouds on the Piranha Plant Pipeway track are just recolored bushes, which is a nod to the original Super Mario Bros., where the bushes and clouds are the same art in different colors.

- The Super Mario Kart handbook actually encourages players to look at their opponents' screens, which today is usually considered cheating.

Literary Labyrinth

A maze-like bookstore has opened in Hangzhou, China. The store itself is like something out of the pages of fiction, with mirrored ceilings that make it seem as if the bookshelves reach twice as high, and reading rooms that seem like jungles. There's even an indoor roller coaster and merry-go-round!

Natural Masterpieces

Living Root Bridge

For 125 years, residents near West Sumatra, Indonesia, have crossed Jembatan Akar—a bridge constructed from living tree roots that's over 80 feet long! With the bridge suspended 10 feet above a fast-flowing river, the two trees located on either side were planted in 1890, and it took about 30 years before the bridge was sturdy enough to cross. Today the bridge facilitates trading and tourism.

Hidden Glacier

Photographer David Kaszlikowski used a quadcopter drone to find the perfect place for this glacial photo. Without the drone, he never would have been able to scout the treacherous landscape around K2, the second tallest mountain peak in the world, before embarking on the climb himself.

❯ The Door to Hell, a large burning crater 230 feet in diameter in the desert of Turkmenistan, has been on fire for over 40 years!

❯ In space, there's a massive reservoir of water floating next to a black hole.

Uncommon Traditions

Lucky Cats

A temple in Tokyo houses one thousand *Maneki Neko* ("lucky cat") statues. In Japan, lucky cats are said to bring good fortune to people who put them in their homes or businesses. This stems from a folktale in which a cat attracts a wealthy noble to a struggling temple.

Mud People

Every year, villagers from Bibiclat, Nueva Ecija Province, Philippines, wear capes of dried banana leaves and cover themselves in mud to thank their patron saint, John the Baptist, for all the blessings they receive. This unique ritual has been happening nonstop ever since the Japanese occupation of the Philippines during World War II.

It is customary in Denmark for your friends to throw heaps of cinnamon at you if you turn 25 and are unmarried.

After their baby teeth fall out, many children in Greece toss them onto the roof in hopes of healthy adult chompers.

Taking Flight

Enter the Dragon

North of Beijing lies China's largest dam, where an 846.5-foot-long escalator in the shape of a giant dragon spans across the Longqing Gorge. The serpentine escalator takes visitors up to the top of the dam and is actually the world's largest outdoor escalator. Unfortunately, the trip only takes visitors up and not back down.

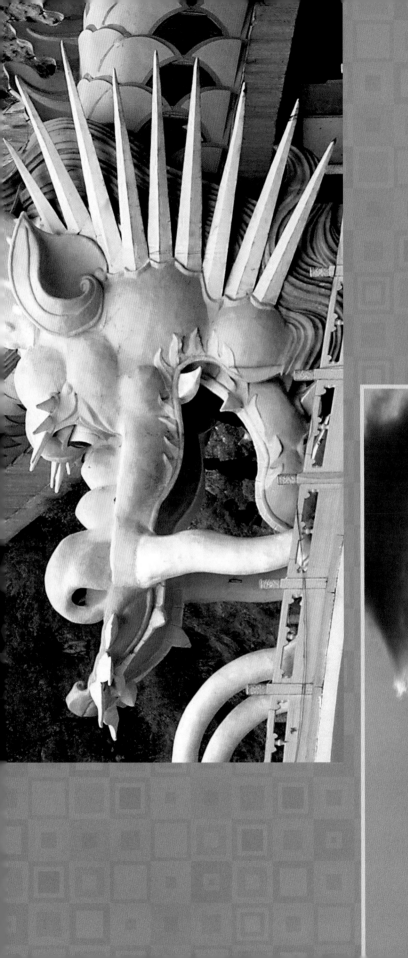

Sky Dragon

On April 22, 2015, a cloud shaped like a fire-breathing dragon appeared over Briones Regional Park in California. This was just in time for England's celebration of St. George's Day on April 23. According to legend, St. George fought in the Roman army, rescued a princess, and famously slayed a dragon.

Odd Events

True Grits

The World Grits Festival in South Carolina includes a competition to see who can cover themselves in the most grits by rolling in a pool of traditional Southern goodness. The contest begins once the grits pool, which tips the scales at 2,500 to 3,000 pounds, is filled. The objective is simple: all participants get weighed before and after rolling in the grits, and whoever gains the most grit weight is crowned the winner.

Five **CRAZY COMPETITIONS**

1

PLENTY OF HOOPLA Over 200 seniors of Wellesley College's class of 2003 participated in the 107th annual hoop rolling contest on the grounds of the campus.

2

BUG OUT The Story Bridge Hotel in Brisbane, Queensland, Australia, has hosted the Cockroach Race on Australia Day (January 26) for 36 years! Entrants can either bring their own cockroach or purchase one on game day.

3

SPEED DREAMS The Great Knaresborough Bed Race sees 630 participants race decorated beds over a challenging 2.4-mile course.

4

NO STRINGS Contestants at air guitar competitions play for 60 seconds while judges mark them on technical ability and stage presence.

5

WORM CHARMING Every year at the World Worm Charming Championships in Willaston, England, competitors try to coax the most earthworms up to the surface.

Different Dwellings

Urban Treehouse

One eco-friendly apartment building in Turin, Italy, is making for happy—and healthy—neighbors. Completed in 2012, the 63-unit complex contains 150 potted trees integrated within the building's structure. The greenery creates its own microclimate, protecting the residents from both air and noise pollution.

Mind Your Head

This tiny Welsh house is six feet wide and can only fit four people inside. Dubbed the smallest house in Britain, this Conwy cottage housed a lone fisherman who spent most of his time out on the water. Now it's a tourist attraction that sees hundreds of visitors every week.

Flipped Home

Believe it or not, this entire house is upside down, inside and out! Created by a group of architects, this pastel-colored home cost $600,000 to create and was on exhibit for five months at Huashan Creative Park in Taipei, Taiwan. Tourists explored the home, walking on the ceiling and taking pictures of everything from the living room fireplace to the kitchen sink, all of which were firmly fastened to the floor above their heads.

Sea of Roses

Over 50,000 yellow and red rose-shaped LED lanterns were arranged in a park in Qingdao, China. The flowers were arranged for the 26th International Beer Festival, and when viewed from above, they are arranged to create a red star surrounded by a golden swirl.

QUIZ

What themed house should you live in?

Pick an ideal place to chill on the weekend:

-or-

Do you like sports?

YES

NO

Do you enjoy nature?

YES

NO

Pick a color!

When it snows you

Pick a color!

At the beach you

PAGE 13
Teapot house

PAGE 36
Urban treehouse

PAGE 18
Psychedelic salt mine

Smallest house
PAGE 37

Croc cage
PAGE 16

Fire football
PAGE 14

Flipped house
PAGE 37

Shell house
PAGE 12

CHAPTER 2

Unreal Animals

Silly Strays

EMUsing Pet

This emu stole the hearts of residents when it wandered into the village of Saperon Ki Dhaani in India. After being rescued from attacking dogs, the flightless bird now hangs out with the village children, who feed and protect their new exotic pet.

Live-In Alpaca

When Little Cody was abandoned by her mother, Amber Isaac brought the animal into her home, and the alpaca hasn't left since! The two do everything together. Cody even climbs upstairs and into Amber's bed at night. Isaac also likes to dress Cody up in different wigs and outfits to post online to Cody's 40,000 fans.

Astonishing Creatures

Greenland Sharks

Greenland sharks live for at least 270 years—maybe as long as 500—and do not reproduce until they are 150 years old. They also grow extremely slowly, at a rate of around 0.4 inches a year.

Assassin Bugs

To protect itself from predators, the Malaysian assassin bug will pile other dead insects on its back to appear bigger and provide camouflage. It first injects its poisonous saliva into the prey and then sticks 20 or more ants or other bugs to its body.

Pink Grasshopper

Photographer John Harding caught this rare pink female grasshopper on camera. The photo, taken in Whitchurch, England, showcases the unique genetic mutation, making this pink hopper a particularly rare sight.

Cuddly Critters

Adopted Bear

Stepan the bear was found alone and weak in the woods when he was just three months old. Russian couple Svetlana and Yuriy Panteleenko nursed him back to health and now, 23 years later, he still lives with them in Moscow, like a cuddly and abnormally large dog. The Panteleenkos say the seven-foot-tall bear loves people and has never shown signs of aggression.

→ Five Wacky Facts about **PETS**

1 **PARTY ANIMALS** Fyodor Romodanovsky, the head of the Russian secret police under Tsar Peter the Great, trained bears to serve guests strong peppered drinks at his parties—and attack them if they didn't drink it!

2 **DOG DAYS** Henry III of France (1551–1589) had 2,000 lap dogs and regularly wore puppies around his neck in a basket.

3 **COOL CANARY** In 1920, 10,000 people lined the streets of Newark, New Jersey, to pay their respects to a local pet canary named Jimmy, who was carried in a coffin by a 500-strong funeral procession complete with 15-piece band.

4 **ELDERLY FISH** A pet koi carp named Hanako was thought to have lived in Japan from 1751 to 1977—226 years!

5 **NINE LIVES** In ancient Egypt, killing a cat—even unintentionally—was punishable by death!

Animal Art

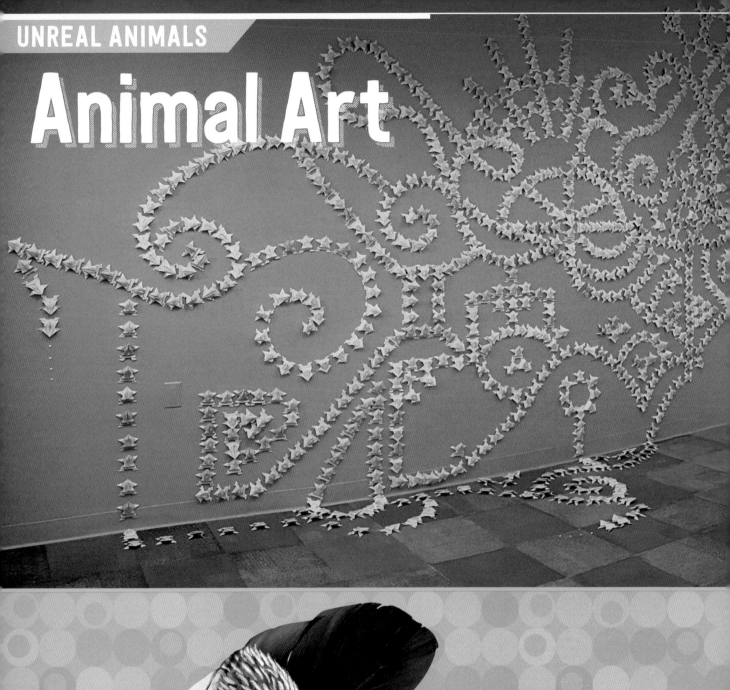

Origami Frogs

In 2016, artist Lara Nguyen, based in North Carolina, folded 1,000 paper frogs in the hopes that her single sister will find true love. She combined the Japanese legend, which says that a person's wish will be granted should they fold 1,000 paper origami cranes, along with the Brothers Grimm fairy tale, "The Frog Prince," to create the 25-foot-wide work, called *Folding Prince Charming*.

Feather Canvas

Artist Krystle Missildine, based in Prattville, Alabama, creates hyper-realistic paintings on bird feathers! Using naturally molted feathers as a canvas is quite challenging, as the individual hairs (called barbs) are small and delicate. Her feather paintings take anywhere from three to 10 hours to complete.

Sea Pals

Surfing Cat

Kuli, a one-eyed cat, regularly goes surfing with owners Alexandra Gomez and Krista Littleton in the ocean off Honolulu, Hawaii. They adopted Kuli (whose name means "to look blind") when he was three months old and weighed just one pound. Today, Kuli is much bigger and stronger, and he has become so adept at riding the waves that he has his own surfboard.

Hang Fin

Whale, whale, whale—what have we here? Surfers were practicing their skills on some waves off the coast of Hermanus, South Africa, when a southern right whale decided to join in on the fun! The massive aquatic mammal got within three feet of the athletes, seemingly enjoying all the attention.

Mesmerizing Mammals

The world's lightest mammal, the Kitti's hog-nosed bat, weighs about as much as two M&M's candies.

Bowhead whales have the largest mouths in nature—bigger than the size of an SUV!

Knockout Kangaroo

Don't mess with Roger the red kangaroo. Roger, who lives at the Kangaroo Sanctuary in Alice Springs, Australia, stands over six feet tall, weighs nearly 200 pounds, and crushes metal buckets with his bare paws. Roger is also trained in hand-to-hand combat and enjoys daily bouts of kangaroo kickboxing.

Mismatched Eyes

Twin cats Iriss and Abyss have beautiful mismatched eyes! They both have the genetic condition heterochromia, which causes the discoloration in their eyes. Owner Pavel Kasianov, from Saint Petersburg, Russia, adopted the kittens after seeing their unique appearance, and has since set up an Instagram account for the cool kitties, which has more than 100,000 followers!

Snow-White Giraffe

Omo the snow-white giraffe from Tarangire National Park, Tanzania, exhibits a remarkable case of leucism, or partial loss of pigmentation. While Omo's distinctive look makes her a glaring target for poachers, Omo is beating the odds. She's survived her first year despite not having the usual camouflage coloring of giraffes.

Dinosaurs

→ The longest complete dinosaur fossil found is an 89-foot-long Diplodocus, which was discovered in Wyoming.

→ Despite the title, most of the dinosaurs from *Jurassic Park* lived during the Cretaceous period.

→ Velociraptors were about as tall as flamingos, and recent research suggests that *Velociraptor mongoliensis* had feathers like many modern birds!

→ The word "dinosaur" comes from the ancient Greek and means "terrible lizard."

→ The 1993 *Jurassic Park* movie has a running time of 127 minutes—but includes only 14 minutes of actual dinosaur footage.

→ Just like crocs and gators today, dinosaurs often swallowed rocks, which helped them grind up food.

→ Villagers in central China have long been using dinosaur bones as medicine, originally believing they were from dragons.

→ In 2015, a four-year-old searching for fossils in Texas found 100 million-year-old dinosaur bones.

→ One of the smallest known dinosaurs was about four inches tall and weighed less than a Chihuahua.

→ The roar of *Jurassic Park*'s T. rex was made by layering elements of tiger, alligator, and baby elephant sounds.

→ Paleontologists know dinosaurs replaced their teeth throughout their life, just like sharks and crocodilians still do today.

→ The raptors in *Jurassic World* were played by real people who were later turned into dinosaurs with computer animation.

Picture Perfect

Fire-Breathing Stag

Photographed in Bushy Park, London, this stag appears as if it's breathing fire. Captured by photographer Norman Crisp, the "fire" is actually the sun's rays shining through the creature's misty breath during the cold morning. Crisp was stunned when he later saw the photo. He hadn't noticed the image's fantastic appearance when he took the photo.

Incredible!

Macaque monkeys in Thailand have been observed teaching their young to floss using human hair!

Time of Our Lives

Swamp tour guide Lance Lacrosse, aka the Alligator Whisperer, gets up close and personal with wild alligators in the murky waters of Louisiana, even lifting one up *Dirty Dancing*–style. The 29-year-old plays and swims with the alligators who come close enough to take a bite out of him. Unbelievably, Lacrosse has been swimming with gators since he was nine years old.

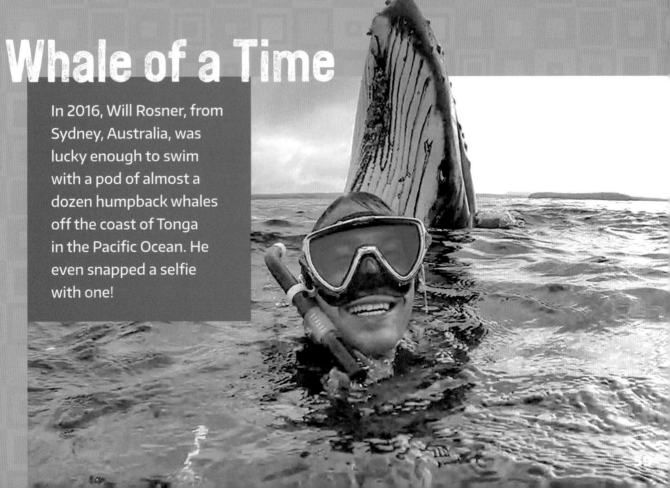

Whale of a Time

In 2016, Will Rosner, from Sydney, Australia, was lucky enough to swim with a pod of almost a dozen humpback whales off the coast of Tonga in the Pacific Ocean. He even snapped a selfie with one!

Elephant Rescue

This young elephant in Kenya became stuck after falling into a mud pit while trying to get a drink of water. After spending up to 12 hours in the ditch, the massive mammal was able to escape. That's when conservationists and construction workers teamed up, using an excavator to create a gentle slope that allowed him to walk up and out of the scary situation.

One in a Million

Vampire Giraffe

A trio visiting a nature reserve in Limpopo, South Africa, snapped this photo of a giraffe with what appears to be long, sharp fangs! After observing the unusual vampire for a while, the tourists realized the "teeth" were actually part of a bone the long-necked mammal was chewing on.

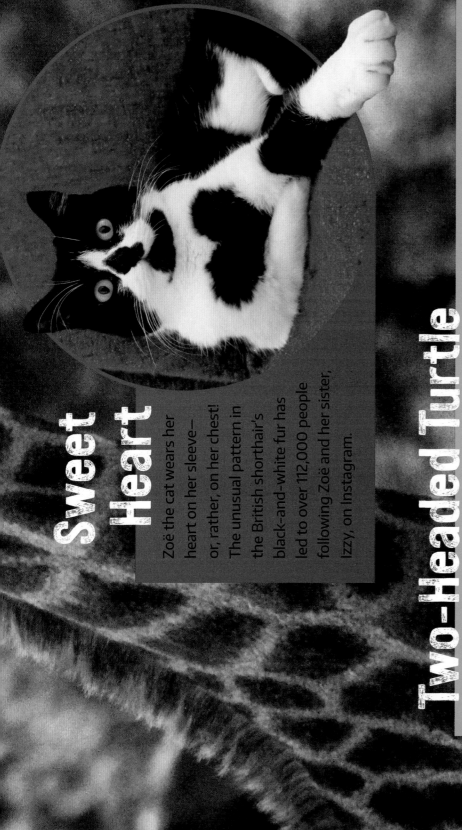

Sweet Heart

Zoë the cat wears her heart on her sleeve—or, rather, on her chest! The unusual pattern in the British shorthair's black-and-white fur has led to over 112,000 people following Zoë and her sister, Izzy, on Instagram.

Two-Headed Turtle

Jeo Armansary, from Jakarta, Indonesia, owns a red-eared slider turtle that has two heads and four eyes. The turtle is able to eat normally with both heads moving independently of each other.

Free as a Bird

Feathered Friend

In 2015, residents of Noordeinde, a small town in the Netherlands, spotted a stray Eurasian eagle-owl. They think the six-pound bird might have escaped from a nearby aviary. The outgoing owl made some new friends by landing on a few unsuspecting people's heads!

Five Silly Facts about **BIRDS**

1 **DARK CHICKEN** The Ayam Cemani chicken of Indonesia has black feathers, a black beak, black skin, and even black organs!

2 **VOMITING VULTURES** The turkey vulture vomits the foul-smelling contents of its stomach at predators.

3 **SPIKED SHELTER** The Chihuahuan raven uses more than just twigs to build its nest—some use paper, cloth, and even barbed wire!

4 **FLIGHTY PILOT** During World War II, the U.S. government experimented with bombs steered by pigeons!

5 **MASTER OF DISGUISE** The nocturnal common potoo bird of South America pretends to be a tree branch during the day and can see through closed eyelids!

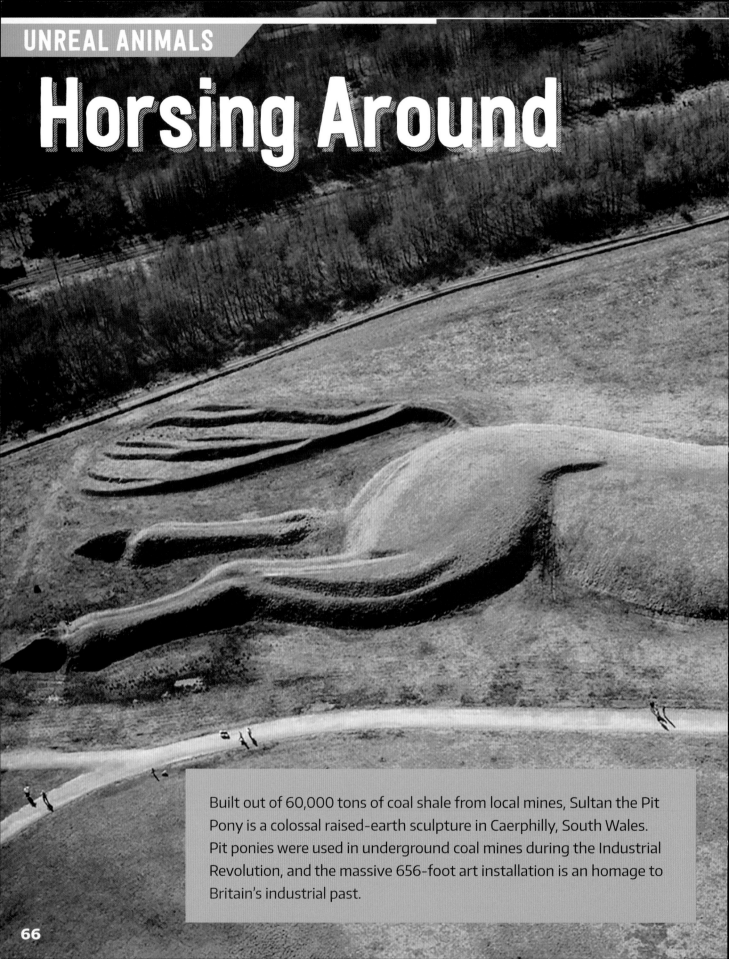

Horsing Around

Built out of 60,000 tons of coal shale from local mines, Sultan the Pit Pony is a colossal raised-earth sculpture in Caerphilly, South Wales. Pit ponies were used in underground coal mines during the Industrial Revolution, and the massive 656-foot art installation is an homage to Britain's industrial past.

Crawling Art

Los Angeles artist Steven Kutcher uses insects as living paintbrushes. He takes flies, cockroaches, and beetles in his hand and adds paint onto each leg, one leg at a time. He then releases them onto a prepared canvas, allowing them to create a trail of color. To ensure his insects come to no harm, he always uses water-based, nontoxic paints that wash off easily.

Q *How long have you been doing bug art?*

STEVEN KUTCHER: I started experimenting in 2003 and originally wanted to make shoes for the insects so their footprints would be larger, but I figured out how to enlarge the insects' footprints on paper.

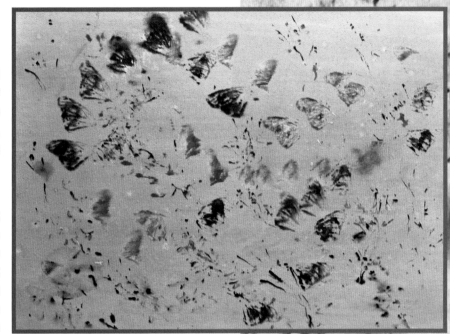

Why use bugs to paint?

SK: The world is covered with insect footprints and most are invisible, so I decided to make those footprints visible. I studied insect behavior at college and wanted to investigate the movements of insects. I liked the idea of combining art and science and using insects.

Have you ever thought about doing the same thing with other animals?

SK: No, but if I did, I would use animals with delicate feet like a vireo [bird] or large animals—like elephants, camels, or buffalo—on a large format. Beetles are easier to get and keep than giraffes.

Do you keep the bugs as pets or are they released into the wild?

SK: I keep them in my bug zoo, and they have a good life with plenty of food and housing. When beetles are caught in the wild, you do not know how old they are, but beetles live up to five years in captivity.

How do you handle the bugs? Do you wear gloves?

SK: Having a delicate touch is extremely important when handling insects. Your grip must be strong enough to hold the beetle but not too strong that you damage it, since it has a hard exoskeleton. When I first started, I used my bare hands. Now, I have found it more convenient and less messy to use latex gloves.

How long does it take you to complete a typical piece?

SK: The background may take a number of hours or days to complete. When I first started, it was one session of one to three hours. I know how to paint better, so one painting may take place over a number of weeks or months, but now a significant part of the painting is done in one or two sessions.

How do you keep flies from flying away?

SK: By putting lots of paint on their feet.

Saving the Day

Super Sniffers

Heroic rats are saving thousands of people every year, one sniff at a time. Specially trained African giant pouched rats, also known as HeroRATs, can detect dangerous and potentially deadly landmines. The brave rodents can search 2,152.8 square feet in 20 minutes—humans with mine detectors would need 25 hours to search the same area!

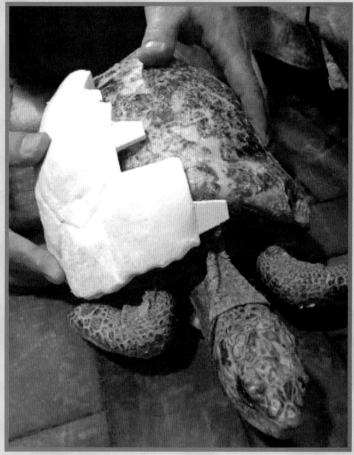

Printed Shell

Freddy the tortoise was in bad shape after a forest fire in Brazil destroyed most of her shell. Luckily, a group of volunteers known as the "Animal Avengers" were able to restore her to her former glory by using 3-D printing technology. Her new shell is made up of four pieces of corn-based plastic, each of which took 50 hours to print! An artist then painted the assembled shell to look like a real one.

Penguin Mouths

Penguin mouths are lined with fleshy spikes to help guide food toward their stomachs. Since the fishy feasts are usually still wriggling when they get swallowed, the backward-facing spines make sure the meal stays down!

On Middle Island off the coast of Victoria, Australia, Maremma sheepdogs protect a colony of the world's smallest penguins from predators.

Penguins have a gland above their eyes that removes salt from their blood.

QUIZ

Which animal should be your sidekick?

Pick your favorite kind of snack:

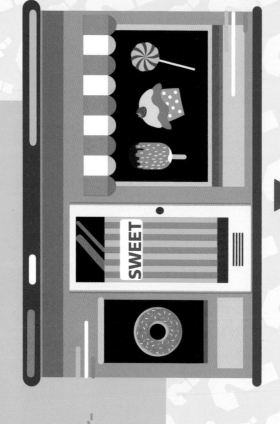

SWEET

-or-

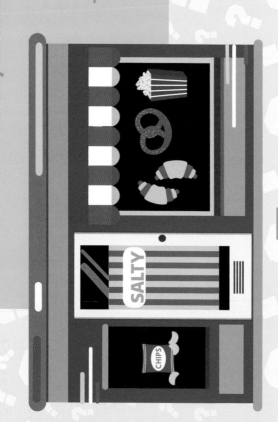

SALTY

Do you like art?

NO

YES

Do you enjoy climbing trees?

NO

YES

Favorite weather

☀ ▭

PAGE **48**
Stepan the bear

PAGE **52**
Surfing cat

How you get there

🚗 ✈

PAGE **44**
Friendly emu

PAGE **45**
Cody the alpaca

Favorite weather

☀ ▭

PAGE **55**
Albino giraffe

Dirty Dancing gator
PAGE **59**

In a new city you

📷 🍽

Artistic insect
PAGE **68**

Two-headed turtle
PAGE **63**

CHAPTER 3

Larger Than Life

Stadium Spectacular

In 2015, James Kingston became the first person to climb on top of the 435-foot arch over London's Wembley Stadium. James, 24, was attached to a wire during the climb. The British man has climbed other impressive structures around the world, including Dubai's second-tallest building, the Princess Tower.

Working It Out

BMX Yoga

Khivraj Gurjar, 65, practices yoga on his BMX bicycle while balancing on a boulder teetering 300 feet above the ground in Rajasthan, India. The senior daredevil spends an hour each day holding 45 different poses on his bike, demonstrating a mastery of balance.

Laundry Lessons

Find your inner peace at Bubbles Launderette in England, where yoga classes are offered alongside the washers and dryers. In addition, Bubbles patrons can enjoy live music and even take French lessons.

Pokémon Go led Americans to take an estimated 144 billion extra steps in the first month of its release alone!

New Jersey massage therapist Dr. Dot uses an unusual technique on her celebrity clients—biting!

Come Together

The Brainy Bunch

Believe it or not, 550 schoolchildren dressed as Albert Einstein in December 2016 at the National Physical Laboratory in New Delhi, India. Hoping to break a world record, the young participants dressed up in Einstein's characteristic white hair and mustache, and each wore a blazer and neck tie.

Five STRANGE GATHERINGS

1 **REMARKABLE REVELRY** November 4, 2016. After the historic Chicago Cubs' World Series win, the celebratory parade—with over five million people in attendance—became the seventh largest gathering in human history!

2 **DEFT DANCERS** September 3, 2011. The largest single-dancer lion dance display was achieved by 3,971 schoolchildren in Taiwan. The performance only lasted about six minutes.

3 **MATTRESS MANIA** July 23, 2016. The largest human mattress domino chain—where each person holds onto a mattress and falls onto the next person—consisted of 2,016 participants and mattresses in Hubei, China.

4 **HE CAN MULTIPLY!** October 30, 2015. A Rooms To Go in Seffner, Florida, held the largest gathering of people dressed as Peter Pan—289.

5 **MAGICAL MEETING** March 5, 2015. The largest gathering of people dressed as Harry Potter—521 muggles wearing wizard hats, Hogwarts uniforms, and glasses—happened in West Sussex, United Kingdom.

Brave Balancing

Highline walkers Lukas Irmler and Samuel Volery balanced their way across an 886-foot-long slackline strung across Mount Pilatus in Switzerland. Braving heavy fog, wind, and rain, the daredevils finished their journey in about 50 minutes.

Strange Kitchens

Tough Hands

Cook Prem Kumar, from New Delhi, India, can fry fish by dunking them in hot oil with his bare hands! Thanks to the Leidenfrost effect—when a liquid in close contact with something hotter than its boiling point produces an insulating vapor—moisture on his hands vaporizes into steam in the boiling oil, forming a protective barrier around his hand for short periods at a time. Definitely don't try this at home!

Creepy Crawly Cookery

English student Courtney Yule designed a kit to help people turn insects into food! When Yule learned about the many benefits of eating bugs, she created the Entopod—a kitchen tool that grinds insects into a powder. It also includes detachable containers for microwave and oven cooking and even a fondue pot for dipping insects into melted cheese or chocolate!

LARGER THAN LIFE

→ Taylor Swift was the first *Saturday Night Live* host to ever write his or her own monologue, a song that included jabs at Joe Jonas and Kanye West.

→ At age 14, Taylor was the youngest songwriter to be hired by Sony/ATV Music Publishing house.

→ In 2010, 20-year-old Taylor became the youngest artist in history to win a Grammy Award for Album of the Year.

→ Certified seven times platinum, her album *Fearless* is the most awarded album in the history of country music.

→ "Blank Space" is the most viewed music video by a female artist ever.

→ At 18, Taylor became the youngest sole writer and singer of a number one country song through her single "Our Song."

→ In June 2015, Taylor Swift challenged Apple, a $750 billion dollar company, by making it change its decision with regard to royalty payments to artists during the three-month trial period of Apple Music.

→ Taylor is the only artist in the history of music to have an album hit the 1 million first week U.S. sales figure three times—*Speak Now* (2010), *Red* (2012), and *1989* (2014).

→ She's the first artist since the Beatles (and the only female artist in history) to log six or more weeks at number one in the United States with three consecutive studio albums.

→ Taylor Swift has the second highest number of Instagram followers, with 96.4 million followers as of January 20, 2017.

TAYLOR SWIFT

Rare Necessities

Flying Saucer

In 2011, 46-year-old Chinese farmer Shu Mansheng successfully flew his homemade flying saucer for more than 30 seconds. Powered by eight motorcycle engines and a propeller, he spent only $3,000 building the 18-foot-diameter octocopter.

Incredible!

The first sunglasses in China were worn by judges to hide their emotions.

中国 学校 中国 "太空" 学校

Robot on Aisle Five!

It's not science fiction—robots may soon be bagging your groceries. An architect at the Massachusetts Institute of Technology designed a series of robots nicknamed "YuMi" for Coop, an Italian supermarket chain. The two-armed bagger bots come equipped with pressure sensors designed to keep your produce and eggs safe from squishing.

Whatever the Weather

Do you wish you could ride your bike in any type of weather? So did Portuguese engineer and cyclist Manuel Brito. Manuel created the Leafxpro clip-on windshield, an open plastic windshield that allows cyclists to pedal through rain, snow, and gusty winds.

Extreme Endeavors

Gravity-Defying Grads

College graduates from Hubei Province, China, took part in a special photo shoot to celebrate their academic accomplishments. The goofy grads used a walkway under water in a flooded lakeside park, giving the illusion that the scampering scholars were running on water!

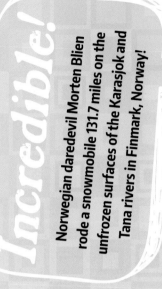

Incredible!

Norwegian daredevil Morten Blien rode a snowmobile 131.7 miles on the unfrozen surfaces of the Karasjok and Tana rivers in Finmark, Norway!

Crazy Cuts

Russian barber Denis Yushin travels the world on a motorcycle, funding his adventures by offering haircuts in extreme locations. The "motobarber," as he is known online, has trimmed hair under the sea, on top of a volcano, and even 1,000 feet in the air while paragliding!

Arctic Daredevil

California's Ben Stookesberry is the first person to plummet over a glacial waterfall in a kayak. Ben, 34, braved the 65-foot drop during a 2012 expedition to Svalbard, Norway, above the Arctic Circle. Ben spent four-and-a-half days traveling to the waterfall and wore a special suit designed to prevent hypothermia.

Below the Surface

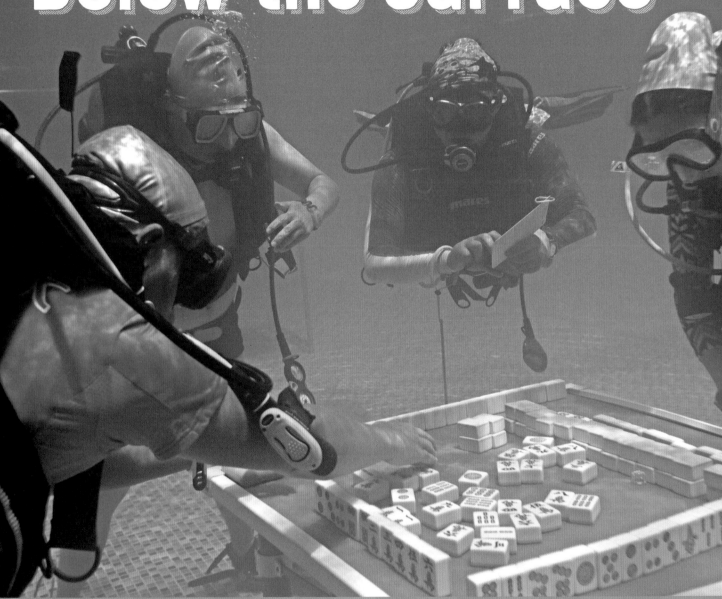

Underwater Mahjong

In August 2016, nine people competed in the 300-year-old game of mahjong underwater in Chongqing, China. The players were outfitted in diving gear to play seven feet below the surface of the water. Underwater matches last up to two or three times as long as normal games of mahjong, and participants are exhausted by the finish.

Five UNDERWATER ACTIVITIES

1 SLIPPERY SMACKDOWN
Underwater octopus wrestling in Washington's Puget Sound was a popular sport in the 1960s.

2 STRANGE GAME
"Octopush" is a type of hockey played underwater in South Africa!

3 OIL IN WATER
Belgian scuba diver Jamy Verheylewegen creates oil paintings while underwater and exhibits his work in swimming pools!

4 STEAM CLEAN
The sport of extreme ironing sometimes includes ironing underwater.

5 ROUGH WATERS
In underwater rugby, players—who wear flippers, snorkels, and goggles—try to place a ball filled with saltwater in the opposing team's basket on the floor of a swimming pool.

Human Towers

At the Tarragona Castells Competition in Spain, teams consisting of dozens of people compete to form the largest and most complex tower they can build out of their own bodies. Practiced since the 18th century, human towers can reach heights of over 50 feet.

Unbelievable Bodies

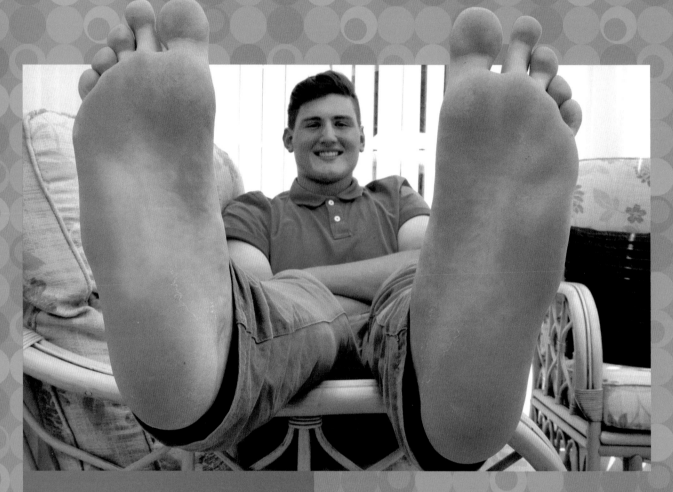

Foot Feat

Fifteen-year-old Sam Preston's feet are 14 inches long . . . and counting. A size UK 19 (US 20), Sam is on track to break the current British record of size UK 21 (US 22). The 6'6" teenager has already surpassed NBA star LeBron James and Olympic swimmer Ian Thorpe in foot size!

Incredible!

Women have twice as many pain receptors on their body as men—but a much higher pain tolerance.

That's a Mouthful

This father-daughter duo has the widest tongues in the world! Byron Schlenker's tongue measures a whopping 3.37 inches across, and teenaged daughter Emily's stretches 2.89 inches from side to side. The pair realized they had titanic tasters when Emily was working on a school project, and they were completely surprised to find they had such unusual tongues.

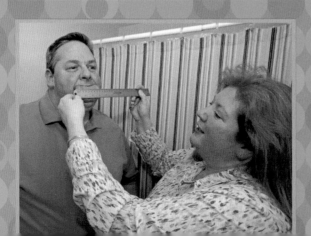

Under the Hood

Start Your Engines

Polish artist Szymon Klimek creates working cars, trains, and steam engines that are smaller than a standard soda can. Klimek crafts the mini machines mostly by hand, using thin sheets of brass and bronze. Some models are powered by tiny solar panels. Klimek designs the miniatures to fit inside glass goblets for display and protection.

Fastest Shed

Kevin Nicks turned a once rusting car into this street-legal shed. Weighing over 2 tons, the shed can speed down the highway at over 70 mph. Despite reluctance from the Driver and Vehicle Licensing Agency, a letter to Prime Minister David Cameron got the car through inspection!

Incredible!

A Latvian man drove his Audi into a pool of 3,170 gallons of Coca-Cola and 88 pounds of baking soda to see if it would help get rid of his car's rust!

Dangling Dancers

The American Bandaloop dance troupe turns the dance floor on its side by performing while suspended by wires, incorporating climbing and cables into their routine. Dangling from the Guigu Cliff in Tianmenshan National Forest Park in China, the performers leapt and spun in sync while hanging high above the ground.

Determined Individuals

Heavy Head

You won't see Cong Yan's form of exercise at your local gym anytime soon. To lose weight, the 54-year-old from Jilin, China, started taking daily walks while balancing a large stone on his head. He started out with a 33-pound rock, which has since moved up to 88 pounds! He walks up to 1.9 miles every day and has shed 66 pounds.

Feel the Gurn

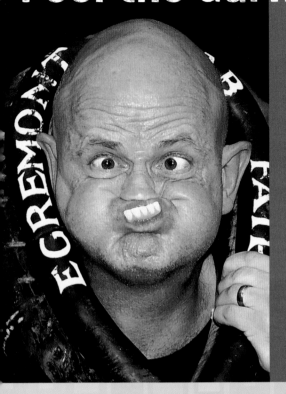

Every September at the Egremont Crab Fair in England, competitors wearing horse collars face off in an effort to be crowned "King of the Gurn" at the World Gurning Championships. Gurning is twisting and contorting the face into ugly expressions—the uglier the better. Believe it or not, the fair was first held in 1267!

Mark of Devotion

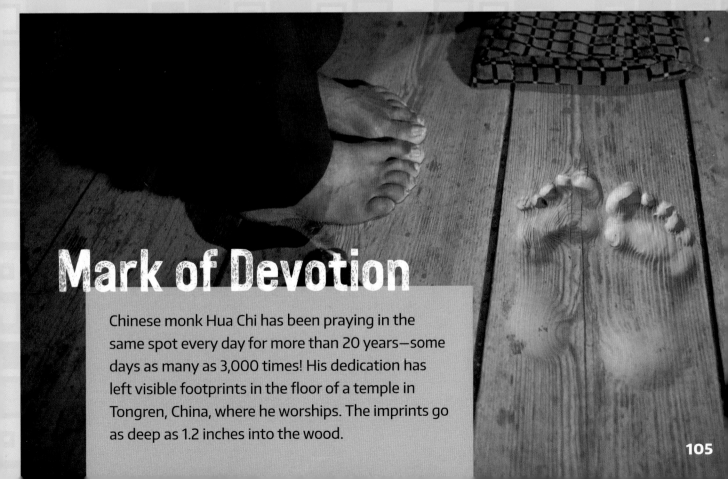

Chinese monk Hua Chi has been praying in the same spot every day for more than 20 years—some days as many as 3,000 times! His dedication has left visible footprints in the floor of a temple in Tongren, China, where he worships. The imprints go as deep as 1.2 inches into the wood.

Skating Free

Kanya Sesser was born without legs and orphaned at just one week old, but that hasn't slowed her down. She's embraced her body and become a basketball player, surfer, and model. Instead of a wheelchair, she prefers to get around by skateboard and is currently training to represent America in the 2018 Paralympics.

Q+A

Q *What drew you to learn skateboarding and surfing?*

KANYA SESSER: As a kid, I was very fascinated with anything that was adventurous and gave me an adrenaline rush. I also had a lot of friends who were into sports. My first time skateboarding was on my friend's board, skating down the hills in our neighborhood, and I loved it! When the Tualatin, Oregon, surfing team saw me at the skate park, they wanted me to come out and surf with them at Cannon Beach, Oregon. It was very cold on my first time ever surfing at age 9.

How long did it take you to master?

KS: My surfing instructor says I was a natural. It took me a month or two to really be comfortable. As for me not having any legs, it takes a lot of power and strength paddling out there in the current, and I sometimes need help pushing out or else the waves would just take me as the swell breaks.

What is the biggest challenge you've encountered living without legs?

KS: I see myself not just as the half-girl or the girl with no legs. I express myself in more meaningful ways. I think my challenge is to show others how independent I am as a person and to teach people that I do not need to be dependent on others.

Are there people you admire? If so, who?

KS: I admire my all-time idol Bethany Hamilton. I don't see her as an armless person surfing. I really appreciate how she still got back out on the board surfing after her incident.

Is there a question you wish people would ask you? If so, what is it and what is your answer?

KS: "What would you say to inspire a group of college students to live life on a higher level despite adversities?" Be the change, make history, express your knowledge and great value. Follow your heart and mind on how you want to help, educate, and teach people. Do it because you love it, not because you have to.

QUIZ

What should you be when you grow up?

Pick where you'd rather go:

-or-

Do you like collecting things?

YES

NO

Do you enjoy solving puzzles?

YES

NO

Favorite time of day

🌙 ☀️

Robot engineer
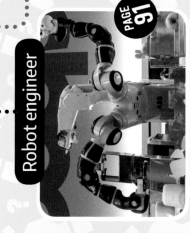
PAGE 91

Helpful inventor

PAGE 91

When bored you

🏃 🖍️🖍️🖍️

Fearless dancer
PAGE 102

Professional skateboarder
PAGE 106

Favorite time of day

🌙 ☀️

Yoga instructor

PAGE 81

Car builder

PAGE 100

With money you

Specialty chef

PAGE 87

Traveling barber

PAGE 93

CHAPTER 4

Trending Stories

Kitty Cantina

A university in Hangzhou, China, has opened a restaurant area themed around the Japanese cartoon character Hello Kitty. The canteen is decorated top to bottom with the famous feline, and the public, along with students, can dine there. The place includes areas for karaoke, crane machines, and dating kiosks.

Bizarre Mediums

Caffeinated Colors

Before sitting down to paint, Maria Aristidou brews a fresh pot of coffee, but she doesn't drink it—she paints with it! Looking for a way to freshen up her watercolors, Aristidou uses coffee to portray everyone from Ellen DeGeneres to R2-D2.

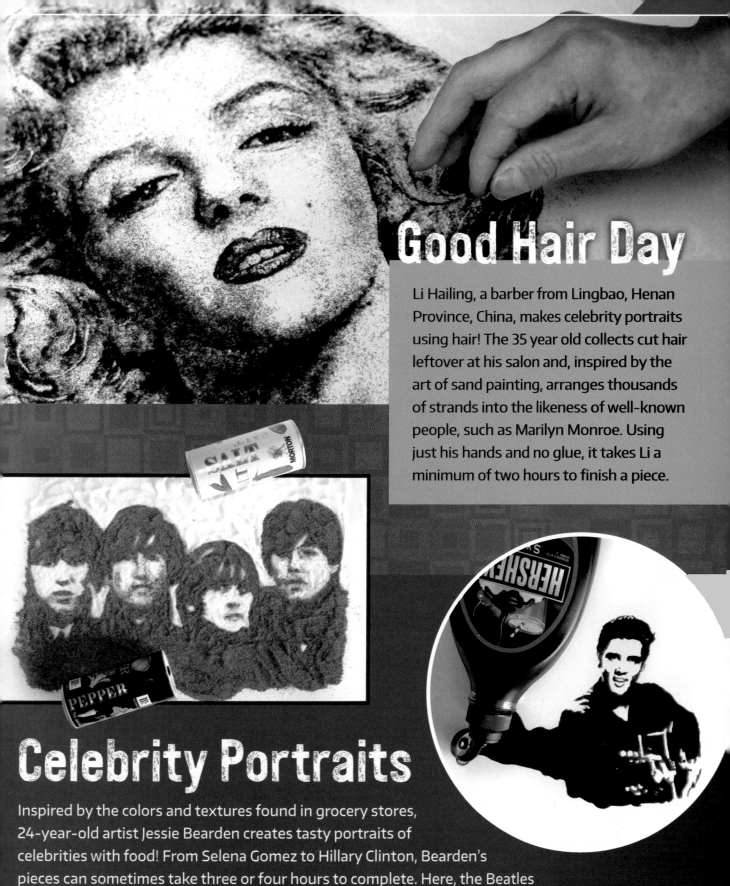

Good Hair Day

Li Hailing, a barber from Lingbao, Henan Province, China, makes celebrity portraits using hair! The 35 year old collects cut hair leftover at his salon and, inspired by the art of sand painting, arranges thousands of strands into the likeness of well-known people, such as Marilyn Monroe. Using just his hands and no glue, it takes Li a minimum of two hours to finish a piece.

Celebrity Portraits

Inspired by the colors and textures found in grocery stores, 24-year-old artist Jessie Bearden creates tasty portraits of celebrities with food! From Selena Gomez to Hillary Clinton, Bearden's pieces can sometimes take three or four hours to complete. Here, the Beatles are made of salt and pepper and Elvis Presley is made of Hershey's chocolate syrup.

Small World

Artist Matthew Carden, from California, created his *Small World* photography series using food! The miniature scenes feature tiny figurines interacting in lifestyle and farming settings, which are entirely edible.

Q+A

Q *When your* Small World *is displayed in a gallery, is it just the photography or is it the actual food scene itself?*

MATTHEW CARDEN: Just the images. There has been a lot of talk about this with a few exhibitions, but the "illusion" I try to create can be ruined by the reality of the tiny scene. It's really small, and the food does not last long. I shoot on location and in studio, but the set is always under 2 x 2 feet. My work is unique in the perspective and approach, and I really try to blur the lines from the reality of the situation I am actually shooting.

Do you set up the image series by yourself (including buying and cooking any food)?

MC: I buy and set up everything, but I have the huge asset of my lovely wife, who has done professional food styling for the past 15 years for me and other photographers. The food I use is usually specific to a region or concept, and sometimes certain items are difficult to find. Some of the food requires no prep, but for food that does, my wife works on it and I shoot it on a set myself.

Where do you acquire the figurines? Do you order them or hand make them?

MC: I buy them in person at various hobby shops. It helps to see them because detail and gesture are so important. I rarely alter them.

Are the figurines glued down?

MC: I do everything I can to make the figures balance on the set as if they were there acting natural. These tiny figurines are scaled from real human models, so many of them have perfect balance if you are patient and dexterous enough. Others require a tiny knife slit in a bean or a dot of honey on the foot to stay still long enough. . . I have a whole bag of tricks.

117

Treasure Troves

Simpson Assortment

Travis McNall, better known as "Bart" to his friends, has been collecting memorabilia from *The Simpsons* for 26 years! His collection consists of 3,772 different items and is still growing!

Five CRANY COLLECTIONS

1 **AVID READER** President Thomas Jefferson's personal collection of over 6,000 books helped rebuild the Library of Congress after British forces burned the U.S. capitol in 1814.

2 **SWEET WALLPAPER** Over 1,300 different, unopened chocolate bars line the walls of Bob Brown's basement in Fishers, Indiana.

3 **BARBIE WORLD** Bettina Dorfmann of Düsseldorf, Germany, owns over 15,000 Barbie dolls.

4 **SPACED OUT** Approximately 300,000 unique items make up Steve Sansweet's California collection of *Star Wars* memorabilia; the mega-fan also wrote a 1.2 million-word *Star Wars* guide in 2008.

5 **CUDDLY OBSESSION** Jackie Miley of Hill City, South Dakota, owns over 10,000 teddy bears!

Weird Food

Sweet Tooth

Baker Laura Loukaides, of Hertfordshire, England, creates cakes and other confections that look like completely different meals— including sushi, spaghetti, pies, and this stack of fast food! The only way to tell the difference is to cut inside and take a bite.

Cotton Candy Grapes

In a weird plot twist for grape lovers, scientists have created cotton candy grapes! California plant breeders have combined two different grape species to create a hybrid that tastes just like your favorite carnival treat. Unbelievably, the whole process takes at least six years, and the new grapes don't look or smell like cotton candy at all.

Flavor. It's in our nature.™

Grapery
est | 1996

Produce of U.S.A.

Cotton Candy™
"These Cotton Candy grapes really do taste li... candy! What a fun, healthy way to enjoy eve... favorite flavor from the fair. Let me know if yo...

Jack Pandol
3rd Generation California Grape Grower
email: jackpandol@grapery.biz

PLU 3093

Incredible!

It is considered back luck to eat lobster on New Year's Day because lobsters can move backward!

Black Ice Cream

Those looking for a dark frozen treat on a bright summer day can now enjoy black ice cream! The glacial goody is sold at Morgenstern's Finest Ice Cream shop in New York City. Made with coconut milk and cream, it gets its unique color from activated charcoal, thought to be healthy and cleansing. Fair warning—this ice cream will turn your hands, mouth, teeth, and tongue black.

Superhero Spree

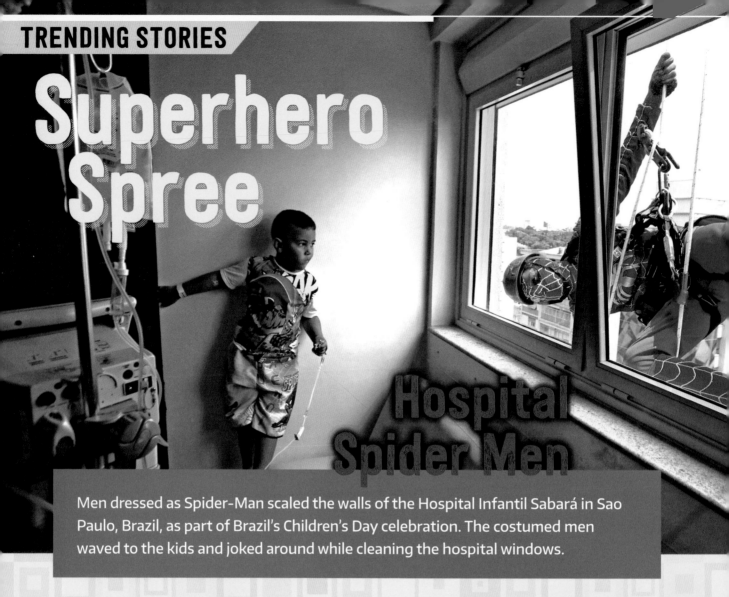

Hospital Spider Men

Men dressed as Spider-Man scaled the walls of the Hospital Infantil Sabará in Sao Paulo, Brazil, as part of Brazil's Children's Day celebration. The costumed men waved to the kids and joked around while cleaning the hospital windows.

Canine Cosplay

Plenty of dog owners play dress-up with their poochy pals, but there aren't many that go as far as Sabrina Ridlon from California. Her patient Doberman pinscher, Penny, is the proud model for this impressive Iron Man costume. All handmade by Sabrina, Penny also has costumes that turn her into a Stormtrooper, a Ghostbuster, and even Batman!

Avenging Art

Orlando, Florida, artist Cristiam Ramos created this 8-foot-tall clay sculpture of Captain America in 2012. Amazingly, it features a colorful collage of the history of superheroes and villains from both Marvel and DC Comics—77 characters total! It took Ramos over six months to create the impressive tribute, as each figure was carved and painted by hand. Can you find these characters: Iron Man, the Flash, Doctor Octopus, the Hulk, and the Joker?

TRENDING STORIES

→ After printing delays on *Daredevil #1*, Stan Lee developed The Avengers, throwing a bunch of existing Marvel superheroes together in a team that would rival DC's Justice League of America.

→ Not everyone wanted to be an Avenger, and in fact, Daredevil and Spider-Man rejected offers of membership.

→ Robert Downey Jr. (who plays Iron Man) kept hiding food on the set of Marvel's *The Avengers*. The crew never found his secret snack stash!

→ One of the few times the full lead cast was in town at once, Chris Evans (who plays Captain America) sent the group a text message simply saying, "Assemble"—a tagline to the movie—prompting a get-together.

→ To prepare for the role of Agent Clint Barton (Hawkeye), Jeremy Renner was trained by Olympic archers.

→ Samuel L. Jackson's role as Nick Fury makes him the second actor (after Hugh Jackman, playing Wolverine) to play the same comic book superhero in seven different movies.

→ Mark Ruffalo's Hulk is the first version of Hulk to have clearly defined chest hair, which has never been done before in any portrayal of Hulk.

→ In the comics, the Wasp actually came up with the name "The Avengers."

→ Despite her youthful appearance, Natasha (Black Widow) is over 70 years old, which explains how she was around during Soviet-era Russia.

→ As of 2015, *The Avengers* surpassed *The Dark Knight*'s record to become the highest grossing comic book film of all time.

AVENGERS

Pop Art
Pebble Portraits

Father and son duo Stefano and Davide Furlani scour the beaches of their hometown Fano, Italy, to find the perfect stones for their rockin' artwork. Young Davide has a knack for picking out interesting pebbles, and together he and his father have recreated famous pop culture characters, such as King Kong, Snoopy, and Elvis Presley!

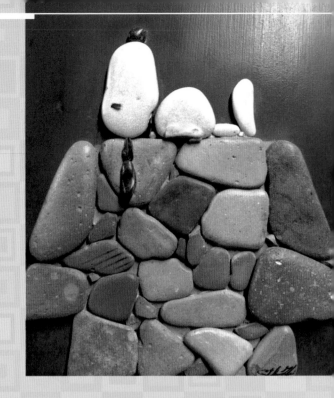

Pooh Illusion

Made by artist Arthur Gugick and acquired by Ripley's, this Winnie the Pooh illusion is made entirely from LEGO blocks! If you view the piece from the right, Tigger is clearly visible, but if you view it from the left, Eeyore and Piglet come into view.

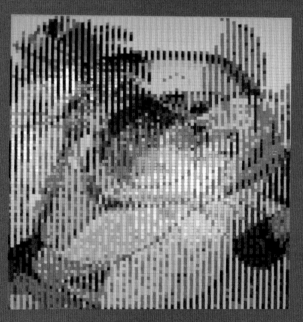

Disney Jigsaw

Amanda Hvilshøj Funch from Copenhagen, Denmark, spent two months completing the world's biggest jigsaw puzzle! The 21-year-old Disney fanatic completed her first 1,000-piece puzzle when she was just seven, but this 40,000-piece giant took a whopping 460 hours to put together. The jigsaw itself is divided into 10 sections, each depicting one classic image from a Disney film.

Well Read

Well of Books

A Chinese mother built a 20-foot-high well-shaped installation with 4 tons of discarded books! The installation, constructed in a café in Shaanxi Province, China, took her about a month to finish. She did it to remind her daughter to never treat reading as a chore—otherwise she would feel like she's mentally confined in a well, rather than being free and open minded.

Five Bizarre Tales about **BOOKS**

1 **SMALL BEGINNINGS** J. K. Rowling wrote her early *Harry Potter* ideas on a napkin while on a delayed train.

2 **SLOW GOING** It took J. R. R. Tolkien 14 years to type all 1,200 pages of *The Lord of the Rings*, partially because he used only two fingers to type!

3 **HEFTY FEE** A copy of *Gone with the Wind* borrowed in 1949 was returned to Rogers High School's library in Spokane, Washington, in 2014—65 years overdue—after the $470 late fee was waived.

4 **LIGHT READING** Working between his heartbeats to keep steady, Vladimir Aniskin of Russia crafted a microscopic book about a flea's shoes.

5 **ROCK SOLID** The Kuthodaw Pagoda in Myanmar contains possibly the largest book in the world, which consists of 730 stone slabs etched with Buddhist teachings.

Artistic Vision

Moss People

Finnish sculptor Kim Simonsson brings Nordic fairy tales to life with these eerie sculptures. Made from ceramic pieces coated in bright green nylon flocking that looks like moss, the sculptures contrast with the environment, yet still have an earthy texture. Simonsson chose to depict figures from Norse mythology that he considers muses for his art.

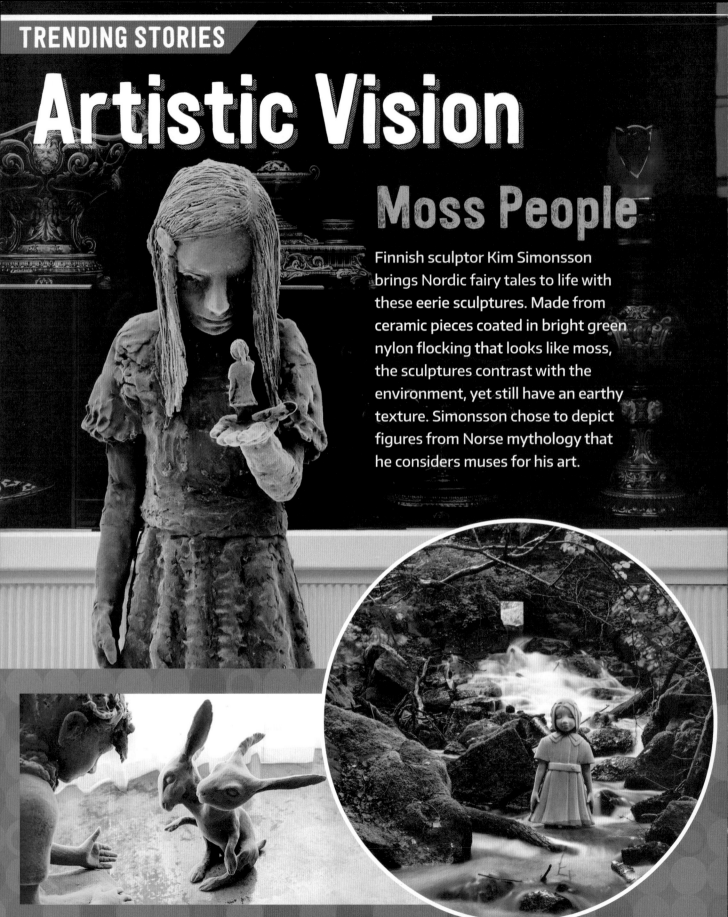

Ghost Clock

On display at the Smithsonian American Art Museum in Washington, D.C., sits what looks like an old grandfather clock covered in a white sheet—but not all is as it seems. Artist Wendell Castle's *Ghost Clock* was hand-carved from a single block of laminated mahogany. That's right—everything from the wrinkled white cloth to the rope are all made from the same piece of wood, tricking the eye in a masterful illusion.

Tiny Violin

Scottish artist David Edwards is a miniaturist, making intricate miniatures of household goods—like this tiny violin! The miniature violin is one of the world's smallest and is handcrafted to one-twelfth the scale of a Stradivarius violin. Just 1.5 inches long, the little fiddle even has real gut strings.

Peculiar Pieces
Straw Sculptures

Amy Goda uses leftover rice straw to create enormous animal designs. The intricate sculptures are made from the straw leftover from rice harvests in the Niigata Prefecture in Japan and molded around wooden frames to create gigantic animals and dinosaurs.

One Man's Trash

Danish artist Thomas Dambo builds larger-than-life sculptures made out of recycled wood, metal, and plastic. Some of his creations include a giant using a real car as a toy, a massive kangaroo with a pouch you can hang out in, and Big Boss Bertel—a huge sculpture (pictured here) that even has a stairway so you can go up and see through his hat for a better view.

Ready for Battle

Iron Panda

Chinese sculptor Bi Heng created a 23-foot-tall panda wearing Marvel superhero Iron Man's trademark suit. Exhibited in Shenyang, Liaoning Province, China, the Iron Panda has a deeper meaning: the sad panda represents humanity's struggle with nature, while the Iron Man suit is symbolic of human technological advancement.

Kaiju Big Battel

Fans of professional wrestling, classic city-crushing monsters, and Japanese sci-fi and horror special effects (known as *Tokusatsu*) will love the Kaiju Big Battel—a competition where evil villains, alien beasts, and destructive monsters fight within a three-roped arena. Much like a professional wrestling event, costumed performers with comical pop culture names "battel" it out against each other.

Hold Your Horses!

This hotel in Chongqing, China, has placed a brightly painted six-foot-tall horse outside of each room's window. The horses stretch six stories into the air, and the colorful artwork helps highlight both the spectacular hotel and a zoo-themed café below.

Horse hooves and human nails are made of the same protein, keratin.

A horse can produce up to 10 gallons of saliva in a single day.

QUIZ

What should be your new hobby?

Pick a place to live:

-or-

Do you play video games?

 YES

 NO

Do you like going to the zoo?

YES

 NO

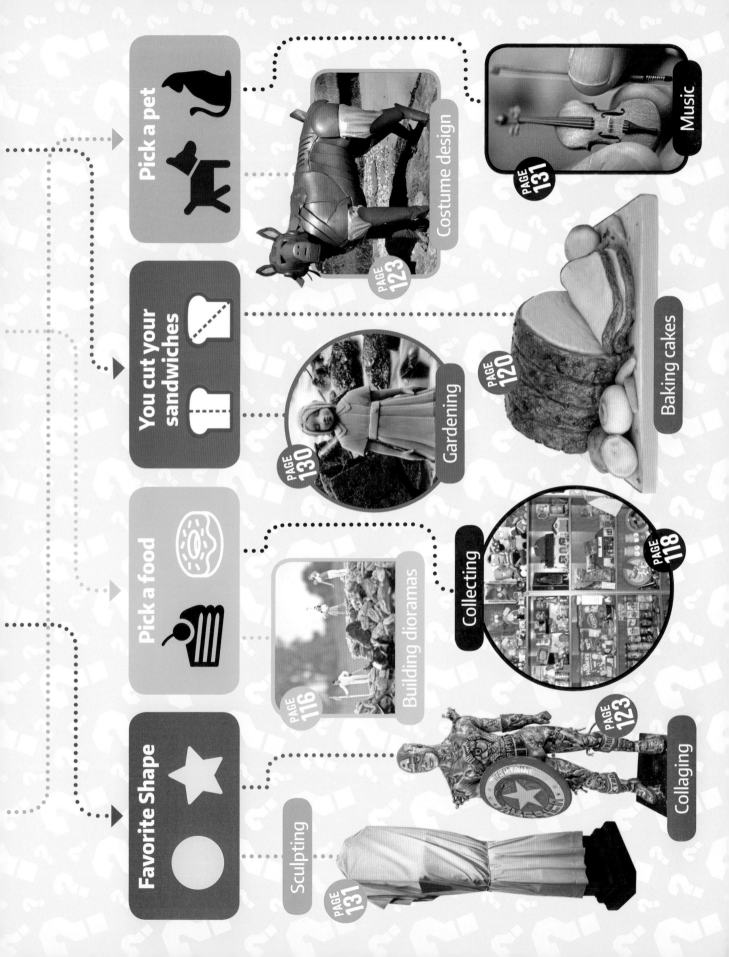

Pick a pet

You cut your sandwiches

Pick a food

Favorite Shape

Costume design
PAGE 123

Music
PAGE 131

Gardening
PAGE 130

Baking cakes
PAGE 120

Building dioramas
PAGE 116

Collecting
PAGE 118

Sculpting
PAGE 131

Collaging
PAGE 123

Ripley Entertainment Inc. and the editors of this book wish to thank the following photographers, agents, and other individuals for permission to use and reprint the following photographs in this book. Any photographs included in this book that are not acknowledged below are property of the Ripley Archives. Great effort has been made to obtain permission from the owners of all material included in this book. Any errors that may have been made are unintentional and will gladly be corrected in future printings if notice is sent to Ripley Entertainment Inc., 7576 Kingspointe Parkway, Suite 188, Orlando, Florida 32819, USA.